D0545701

THE ROYAL HORTICULTURAL SOCIETY
PRACTICAL GUIDES

ROSES

THE ROYAL HORTICULTURAL SOCIETY
PRACTICAL GUIDES

ROSES

Linden Hawthorne

DORLING KINDERSLEY
LONDON • NEW YORK • SYDNEY • MOSCOW
www.dk.com

A DORLING KINDERSLEY BOOK
www.dk.com

PRODUCED FOR DORLING KINDERSLEY BY PAGEOne,
Cairn House, Elgiva Lane, Chesham, Buckinghamshire
PROJECT EDITOR Charlotte Stock
PROJECT DESIGNER Suzanne Tuhrim

SERIES EDITOR Pamela Brown
SERIES ART EDITOR Stephen Josland

MANAGING EDITOR Louise Abbott
MANAGING ART EDITOR Lee Griffiths

PRODUCTION Ruth Charlton, Mandy Innes

First published in Great Britain in 1999
by Dorling Kindersley Limited,
9 Henrietta Street, London WC2E 8PS

Copyright © 1999 Dorling Kindersley Limited, London

All rights reserved. No part of this publication may be reproduced, stored in a retrieval system,
or transmitted in any form or by any means, electronic, mechanical, photocopying, recording,
or otherwise, without the prior written permission of the copyright owner.

A CIP catalogue for this book is available from the British Library.
ISBN 0 7513 0689 4

Reproduced by Colourscan, Singapore
Printed and bound by Star Standard Industries, Singapore

SCOTTISH BORDERS LIBRARY SERVICE	
005168816	
CBS	20/03/2002
635.933734	4.99
	G

CONTENTS

ROSES IN THE GARDEN 7

An introduction to the many ways in which
roses can be grown in the garden; the different
flower forms, habits, characteristics and
uses of the main rose groups.

CARING FOR YOUR ROSES 29

Choosing, planting and training roses;
how and when to prune the different types;
how to encourage better blooms,
and how to keep plants healthy.

A GALLERY OF ROSES 53

A photographic guide to roses of all kinds.

ROSES IN THE GARDEN

WHAT ARE ROSES?

THE MOST ROMANTIC AND MOST ENDURING of all garden plants, roses have probably been displayed since gardens were first cultivated. They have certainly been grown for many centuries, prized not only for the ornamental beauty of their exquisite, often supremely fragrant flowers, but also for hips, leaves and roots used for medicinal purposes and, of course, for their scented oils – Attar of Rose is still used to lend distinctly feminine notes to modern perfumes. In today's gardens, roses are, quite simply, indispensable.

THE ROSE FAMILY

The genus *Rosa*, one of the largest in the plant family Rosaceae, comprises about 150 species of deciduous and semi-evergreen shrubs, climbers and ramblers. Driven by their enthusiasm for roses, plant breeders have created thousands of cultivars. A few of the roses grown today existed in pre-Roman times and would have been easily identifiable in medieval monastery gardens, but the majority were developed from the mid-1700s onward. Breeding programmes continue unabated and, each year, new roses of almost every size and type are introduced, to scent and decorate even the smallest of modern plots.

FRAGRANCE AND BEAUTY
A modern rose, the cluster-flowered Fragrant Delight *combines classic beauty with delicious perfume, both of which can be enjoyed throughout summer.*

◀ ROSE SHOWER *A garden path beneath a tunnel of roses is showered with colour and perfume.*

WHY GROW ROSES?

Few gardens, regardless of their scale or style, fail to benefit from the addition of a rose. Once you learn more about roses and grow to love them, just one or two will seldom be enough to satisfy you.

Roses come in such diverse forms that their uses in gardens are limited only by the imagination. The traditional treatment of large- and cluster-flowered bush roses (Hybrid Teas and Floribundas) as bedding plants is the simplest way of using them – their upright habit is well suited to formal plantings. However, their versatility as a group extends beyond being displayed in flower beds devoted solely to roses.

Shrub roses, both ancient and modern types, are ideal in mixed borders. They associate particularly well with other fragrant shrubs like *Philadelphus* (mock orange), and with summer-flowering bulbs and perennials. Those that are remontant

---

Shrub roses enhance mixed borders of summer bulbs and perennials

---

(repeat-flowering), whether grown alone as specimens or in mixed plantings, will provide glorious colour all summer.

SPECIAL INTEREST

Among more recent developments are roses that are ideal as ground cover. These dense, small-leaved shrubs effectively block out the light beneath them and can make good weed suppressors. Trailing ground-cover roses are ideal for clothing sunny banks, cascading over terrace walls, or even for growing in containers. For the smallest gardens, choose the relatively new patio or miniature roses, which give tremendous

COOL ELEGANCE
Iceberg *is ideal as a specimen or for low hedging. Its graceful habit and clusters of creamy-white flowers complement this mixed planting in shades of silver and blue.*

◀TRADITIONAL
ROSE GARDEN
*Obelisks joined by
fragrant swags of
roses grown on ropes
rise above a long-
flowering carpet of
Floribundas and
Hybrid Teas, giving
colour and fragrance
all summer long.*

▼ROSY MANTLE
*The bare trunk of
this large tree has
been cloaked by the
repeat-flowering*
Compassion, *which
suits small gardens.*

value within a limited space. They provide
a tailor-made solution for the tiniest of city
gardens, and can be grown in containers
or in open ground, in borders or raised
beds. For confined courtyards, there are
even miniature climbers available.

Let trailing ground-cover roses cascade from hanging baskets

Climbing roses are perfect for clothing
drab or unsightly structures, or for
enhancing large expanses of wall, both
high and low. They can also be trained
on pillars and other ornamental structures
such as pyramids or wigwams to give
height and interest to a garden design.
When trained to form a fragrant arbour,
they can provide a place to pause. The
more rampant ramblers are seen at their
best cascading from the limbs of large
trees, with their stems wreathed in blooms.
  All that most roses ask is sun, fertile
weed-free soil, and adequate moisture
and nutrients; in return, they give great
pleasure over many summer months.

TYPES OF ROSE

THE HORTICULTURAL CLASSIFICATION SYSTEM for roses, developed by the World Federation of Rose Societies in 1976, is now widely accepted. Unlike a botanical classification, which groups plants on the basis of similarities and differences between the form, number and arrangements of flower parts, the horticultural system classifies roses according to their size, habit and flower form, each group of roses being suited to a specific garden purpose.

BUSH AND SHRUB ROSES

With the exception of ramblers and climbers, all roses are classified as bushes or shrubs. A shrub rose is more than 1.2m tall when fully grown; it often has a more natural, arching habit than bushes, and may flower just once or repeatedly. Shrub roses are suitable as single specimens or in mixed plantings in a shrubbery or mixed border. In contrast, bush roses are pruned

DAVID AUSTIN'S ROSES
The so-called English Roses are shrub roses that were bred to combine repeat-flowering qualities of the large- and cluster-flowered bushes with the flower forms, colours and fragrances associated with old garden roses.

to a neat, more or less symmetrical form and seldom grow taller than 1.2m. Nearly all bush roses are repeat-flowering, often over very long periods. They are more useful than shrubs in confined spaces, and look good displayed in formal group plantings such as borders and bedding.

CLIMBERS AND RAMBLERS

Most climbers are repeat-flowering roses, bearing flowers on short shoots that arise from old wood and then on new wood later in the season. They are more stiffly upright in habit than the long flexible-stemmed ramblers, most of which produce clusters of flowers only once on growth made during the previous season.

FLOWER FORMS

The relatively simple flower forms of the species roses have been modified by ongoing selection and breeding to yield a number of quite distinct forms (*see below*). Rose flowers range from single (up to 8 petals) and semi-double (8–14 petals) to double (20 or more petals) and fully double (more than 30 petals). They are borne singly, or in small or large clusters (corymbs), and they may be once- or repeat-flowering. The continuity of flowering varies, not only according to cultivar, but also on how well an individual plant has been fed. Its performance can also be affected by the hours of warmth and sunshine in any given season. Some roses flower almost continuously, others bear repeated flushes and some produce a main flush in early or mid-summer, which is followed by a second, lesser flush later in the season.

The scent of roses also varies in intensity to a surprising degree; a few have little, if any, scent but those that are fragrant may present exotic notes of aniseed, myrrh, apples and other fruity scents, as well as the warm, Attar-of-Rose fragrance found in old garden roses, such as the damasks.

ROSE FLOWER FORMS

FLAT
Usually single, with one set of petals that open flat to display a boss of stamens at the centre. Typically seen in species roses, such as *R. glauca* (*see p.52*).

ROUNDED
Double or fully double flowers with even-sized, overlapping petals forming a bowl-shaped or rounded form, as seen in Tequila Sunrise (*see p.55*).

CUPPED
Open, single to fully double blooms with petals curving upwards and outwards, to cup a central boss of stamens, for example 'New Dawn' (*see p.68*).

ROSETTE
Almost flat, double or fully double flowers packed with small, overlapping, slightly uneven petals, as seen in 'Great Maiden's Blush' (*see p.62*).

HIGH-CENTRED
Semi- to fully double flowers with petals that rise to form a high-centred point. Seen in large-flowered bushes, such as Paul Shirville (*see p.53*).

QUARTERED-ROSETTE
Almost flat, double or fully double flowers arranged into four distinct "quarters", for example 'Duc de Guiche' (*see p.64*).

URN-SHAPED
Semi- to fully double, inner petals curving to an urn shape amid flat outer petals. In large- and cluster-flowered bushes, such as 'Hula Girl' (*see p.58*).

POMPON
Small, rounded, double to fully double flowers, usually in clusters, with masses of small petals. Commonly seen in miniature roses, such as 'White Pet' (*see p.58*).

BUSH ROSES

MOST BUSH ROSES are modern roses; that is, developed since 1867, chiefly by breeders in Scandinavia, Europe and the United States. Early breeders focused mainly on flower form and colour but, in recent years, more attention has been given to improving health, hardiness and disease resistance; many modern roses, especially those in the *Gallery of Roses* (*see pp.53–61*), have all of these attributes. Bush roses can be further subdivided into distinct groups.

LARGE-FLOWERED BUSH ROSES

This group is still referred to by its older name, Hybrid Teas, which indicates its ancestry. The first Hybrid Teas were bred from crossings between Hybrid Perpetuals and Tea roses, which originated in China. From the former, they inherited hardiness and vigour along with large, fragrant flowers of rich colours. The Tea roses bequeathed a reliably repeat-flowering habit, glossy leaves and the high-pointed flower buds that remain beloved by florists.

Modern large-flowered bush roses are freely branching, usually thorny-stemmed shrubs of more or less upright or bushy habit. They bear matt or glossy, mid- to dark green leaves composed of quite large oval or lance-shaped leaflets, often flushed with red or purple when young. Their large flowers, mostly urn-shaped or high-centred, are often fragrant and are borne singly or

> The repeat-flowering habit of Hybrid Teas was a revolution for growers

in clusters of up to three. Since they bear flowers on shoots arising from old wood and, most freely, on new wood, they are usually hard-pruned annually (*see p.38*).

► CLUSTERS OF COLOUR
A typical cluster-flowered bush, Valentine Heart *is noted for its pale pink petals with slightly frilled margins.*

▼ SINGLED OUT
Remember Me *is a large-flowered bush with high-centred blooms of rich copper-orange.*

CLUSTER-FLOWERED BUSH ROSES

Floribundas, or cluster-flowered bush roses, were produced in Denmark at the start of the 20th century. Initially called Hybrid Polyanthas, they are derived from crossing Hybrid Teas with Polyantha roses to produce tough and very floriferous plants.

Cluster-flowered roses provide continuous summer colour

In general, cluster-flowered bushes have an upright, free-branching habit and need only light pruning (*see p.39*). They are often hardier and healthier than large-flowered bushes, and show greater resistance to disease. Their single or fully double flowers, which are usually smaller and borne in large clusters or sprays of up to 25 on both the current season's and last year's stems, make them suited to group plantings of non-stop solid colour.

PEACHES 'N' CREAM
A display of Just Joey's *large, sweetly fragrant flowers of coppery pink and buff is interspersed with the dainty flowers of tobacco plants* (Nicotiana).

UNDERPLANTING ROSES

Although bush roses are traditionally seen with bare earth at their base, they can be underplanted with shallow-rooting perennials (*see below*). Leave the immediate root zone free for routine feeding and mulching.

Catmint (*Nepeta* x *faassenii*) Silver leaves and lavender-blue flowers.

Clematis C. *heracleifolia* 'Wyvale', C. *recta*.

Dianthus Clove-scented pinks combine well with rose scents and colours, especially 'Becky Robinson' ♀, pink and ruby-red laced; 'Bovey Belle' ♀, deep pink; 'Doris' ♀, warm pink; and 'Haytor White' ♀, white.

Geraniums Many, especially 'A.T. Johnson', 'Graveteye' and 'Mrs Kendall Clark', all ♀.

Lavenders 'Munstead' ♀ and 'Hidcote'.

Stachys byzantina Silver-leaved ground cover.

Violas and violettas Especially soft blues, violets and purples, like 'Nellie Britton' ♀, 'Huntercombe Purple' ♀ and 'Prince Henry'.

PATIO AND MINIATURE ROSES

The recent development of patio and miniature roses has helped to resolve the problem of finding roses that suit small plots. Patio roses are scaled-down versions of cluster-flowered bushes; indeed, their alternative name, dwarf cluster-flowered bush, is often preferred by many growers, since it avoids the implication that their use is limited to patio plantings. Patio roses are characterized by compact growth of dense habit and smaller leaves than large cluster-flowered bushes. Few of them are noted for having any scent, but they are valued for their clusters of 3–11 small, single to double flowers which appear reliably in repeated flushes from summer to autumn. Like other small bush roses, they require relatively low maintenance: they do not need the very fertile soil demanded by large roses, and pruning (*see p.40*) amounts to little more than deadheading, along with routine removal of dead wood and thinning if the plants become congested.

> # Of all the roses, miniatures are the easiest to manage in containers

Members of the miniature group are the smallest of all roses, seldom exceeding 35cm in height. Raised from the exquisite China rose, *R.* 'Rouletii', they are tiny – but perfectly formed – in all their parts and flower throughout summer. They bring a splash of colour to even the smallest area, whether grown in containers or used as low hedging or as border edging.

▶ COUNTY ROSE
Cambridgeshire *belongs to the popular series of ground-cover roses known as the County Roses, which are named after English shires.*

▼PERFECT ush Baby
*is able to make it*FIT
*At 15–25cm tall, the miniature rose B*self at *home in the smallest of beds and borders, where it makes excellent edging.*

GROUND-COVER ROSES

With prickly stems and small leaves, ground-cover bush or shrub roses provide effective ground cover by virtue of their very dense habit, which excludes light from the soil surface thereby inhibiting germination of weed seedlings. This does not eliminate the need to carry out pre-planting weed clearance and post-planting mulching (*see pp.34–5*) for truly effective ground cover. These routines are absolutely vital and worth carrying out, especially as weeding by hand beneath such prickly bushes can prove a painful task.

STRIKING DISPLAY
A bold planting of pinks and yellows is enhanced by the crimson-scarlet blooms of the patio rose Festival, *which have paler undersides and random streaks of white.*

Ground-cover roses adopt one of two growth habits; some are spreading bushes, while others are trailing, usually with flower clusters wreathing the entire length of their stems. A few flower once only in summer, but most repeat reliably. They can be used for low bedding and edging but are seen at their best cascading over low walls and banks or the sides of containers.

ROSES FOR CONTAINERS

HOT ORANGES	BRIGHT WHITES	FIERY REDS	PRETTY PINKS
Anna Ford ♥ Patio (*p.58*)	**Kent** Ground-cover (*p.60*)	**Boy's Brigade** Patio (*p.59*)	**Avon** Blush pink to pearl-white, ground-cover
Orange Sunblaze Miniature (*p.59*)	**Snowball** Bright creamy-white miniature rose	**Festival** Patio (*p.59*)	**Little Bo-peep** Patio (*p.58*)
Shine On Orange-pink patio rose	**Swany** ♥ Ground-cover (*p.60*)	**'Fire Princess'** miniature (*p.59*)	**'Nozomi'** ♥ Ground-cover (*p.61*)
Sunseeker Orange-red with yellow eye, patio rose	**'White Pet'** ♥ Patio (*p.58*)	**Red Ace** Crimson miniature rose	**Queen Mother** ♥ Patio (*p.58*)
		Robin Redbreast Patio (*p.58*)	

SHRUB ROSES

THE TERM SHRUB ROSE is a catch-all for large, relatively modern roses that do not fall neatly into other categories, from the Hybrid Musks developed at the start of the 20th century to new types of English rose. Although most, by definition, are taller than 1.2m, they are a diverse group. Habit ranges from upright to gracefully arching, and they bear mostly scented, single to fully double flowers, singly or in clusters, usually repeatedly through summer.

HEDGES AND SPECIMENS

The height, spread and prickly habit make shrub roses perfect for hedging. Best of all are the dense and thorny Rugosa roses, with wrinkled, bright green leaves. Their scented, single or semi-double flowers are produced repeatedly through summer, the later blooms borne at the same time as glowing red, tomato-like hips. Few other hedging plants offer such a long season. They need little maintenance: apply balanced fertilizer in spring and lightly trim to shape each year, in early spring for repeat-flowerers, or after

flowering for once-flowering cultivars. If positioned in a prominent site that can be viewed from several angles, modern shrubs make good single specimens. These roses

***

The tangle of thorny stems make rose hedges difficult to penetrate

***

are not hard to cultivate and relatively problem-free, and you are likely to find it difficult to restrict your choice to just one!

INFORMAL SCREEN
Interspersed with love-in-a-mist (Nigella damascena), *the dense, spreading stems and pale pink, mop-headed flower clusters of* 'Ballerina' *make a colourful low hedge.*

▲ CLIMBING HIGH
*Ideal for training against
a wall, the fruit-scented*
Abraham Darby *has a
vigorous bushy habit, and
may grow up to 1.5m tall.*

◀ SHADES OF GREEN
The greyish-green leaves of
L.D. Braithwaite *offer foliage
interest in a mixed border,
while the fragrant, crimson
flowers add strong colour.*

MIXED BORDERS

Shrub roses are rivalled only by old garden roses (*see pp.18–9*) for planting in mixed borders – and many have the advantage of blooming repeatedly through summer, instead of in a single flush. The modern shrubs known as "English roses", bred by David Austin, provide the best features of both. By crossing modern large- and cluster-flowered roses with selected old garden roses, they offer repeat flowering with the flower form, colour, habit and much-loved scents of old garden roses.

In general, shrub roses are more suited to mixed plantings among shrubs, bulbs or perennials than are other rose groups. This is partly because their shrubby habit makes them more graceful than the rigid, upright bush roses and partly because of their range of colours, softer than the startling, almost fluorescent hues found in other modern roses. Shrub roses have sufficient stature to form a backdrop for low-growing plants and hold their own with other medium-sized or large shrubs. Many of them demand a good, fertile soil for maximum performance. This can be catered for with an annual or twice-yearly feed and a mulch of well-rotted manure (*see pp.34–5*). Most shrub roses need little pruning (*see p.42*) other than to shorten main stems by one-third of their length when dormant or after flowering.

GOOD COMBINATIONS

'Buff Beauty' ♔ Apricot then buff, with deep blue *Geranium himalayense* 'Graveteye' ♔.

Gertrude Jekyll ♔ Deep pink. The blooms complement the blue-flowered, herbaceous *Clematis heracleifolia* 'Wyvale' ♔.

Graham Thomas ♔ Rich yellow, with orange-red *Phygelius capensis* ♔, and yellow-flowered *Viola* 'Irish Molly' beneath.

'Penelope' ♔ The pale creamy-pink blooms go well with the blue-flowered *Campanula lactiflora* 'Prichard's Variety' ♔.

OLD GARDEN ROSES

THIS GROUP INCLUDES some of the most ancient roses known in cultivation – the Albas, Gallicas, Damasks, Centifolias and Mosses – which are of European origin and, with rare exceptions, bloom only once in mid-summer. The group also includes hybrids between European and Oriental roses, like the Chinas, Teas, Bourbons and Portlands, which feature similar characteristics to the old European roses, but bloom repeatedly in summer.

WHY GROW OLD ROSES?

While you may at first think that the once-flowering habit of old roses is a major drawback, as you become more familiar with this group it will seem mean-spirited to fault a plant for having only a single, albeit profuse flush of blooms. If, however, you are resolved to have a non-stop display of flowers throughout the summer, choose from the remontant types such as Bourbon and Portland roses. Early crosses of Chinese with European roses yielded repeat-flowering offspring with much of the grace and fine colour of the older roses. In the 19th century, they captured breeders' imaginations to such an extent that they proved the springboard for the development of modern Hybrid Teas.

There are old roses to suit almost every purpose: beds and borders – especially mixed borders; walls, fences and pillars; and for more adventurous training on pyramids, arbours or other structures (*see pp.46–7*). They have, for the most

▶ SPILLING OVER
An informal hedge of 'Complicata' would suit a naturalistic setting or wildflower garden. Its cascading flowers are attractive to honey bees.

▼ JACOBITE ROSE
The bright creamy-white blooms of R. x alba 'Alba Maxima' relieve the dull grey backdrop of a drab wall.

▲ SOFT FOCUS
The coloured foliage of purple sage enhances a solitary, clear pink bloom of Fantin-Latour.

◄ RIPPLED ROSES
Known as Rosa Mundi, R. gallica *'Versicolor' is ideal for mixed borders. Here, its striped flowers associate with pink geraniums to make a vibrant display.*

part, a graceful, natural habit and often flower so freely that stems bend under the weight. The majority are vigorous, tough, and very hardy, many having been in cultivation for more than 150 years.

Old roses are tough and vigorous, and need minimal care

Although most old roses will thrive on minimal attention, they richly reward a little extra feeding with fertilizer and organic mulches. Some may prove slightly prone to mildew, but are generally healthy.

The flowers range from single to fully double, and some are so crammed with petals that they are packed into "quarters". They unfurl and expand to reveal the purest of shades, from soft clear pink to sumptuous crimson and deepest, velvety maroon-purple. Unlike the more colour-fast modern roses, the dark-coloured old roses fade with good grace, revealing hues and tints of lilac, lavender, violet and grey. As for their fragrances, they are simply the true rose scents against which all others must be measured. From spicy perfumes and heady musks to delicate hints of fresh apples and citrus fruits, the intoxicating aromas of old garden roses provide the perfect excuse to linger in their presence.

RECOMMENDED

FLOWERS
'Boule de Neige' Bourbon (*p.62*)
'Cardinal de Richelieu' ♥ Dark velvety-purple Gallica rose
'Duc de Guiche' ♥ Gallica (*p.64*)
'Empereur du Maroc' Hybrid Perpetual (*p.64*)
'Madame Hardy' ♥ White Damask

FRAGRANCE
'Belle de Crécy' ♥ Deep cerise-pink Gallica rose with intense spicy scent
'Bourbon Queen' Bourbon (*p.63*)
R. x centifolia 'Muscosa' ♥ (*p.63*)
'Great Maiden's Blush' Alba (*p.62*)
'Reine des Violettes' Hybrid Perpetual (*p.64*)

FOLIAGE, HIPS AND THORNS

WHILE HYBRID ROSES OF ALL KINDS are grown and valued primarily for their blooms and long flowering season, it is easy to overlook a number of other sterling garden virtues. The wild or species roses, in particular, along with selections and simple hybrids derived from them, offer beautifully delicate flowers but, in addition, may also have brilliantly coloured, often large or unusually shaped hips, as well as attractive foliage or spectacular thorny stems.

SPECIES ROSES·

Natives of hedgerows and woodland, species roses possess a beauty of quite a different order to that of their highly bred garden cousins. They are admired for their elegantly natural habit of growth, their small-leaved foliage and the simplicity of their mostly single flowers. Species roses meld perfectly into informal or naturalistic plantings, in a wildflower garden or mixed informal hedge. Their ornamental hips also make a splash of colour during winter and provide a welcome source of food for birds in winter. Climbing species roses are seen at their best when doing what comes naturally to them, scrambling up trees and tumbling down in cascades. Wild roses are quite self-sufficient, and require little attention. Other than keeping old plants

Species roses are ideal for mixed hedges or woodland plantings

clear of accumulations of dead wood, they need little in the way of pruning – indeed, minimal pruning is recommended to preserve their natural grace and form.

▲ INCENSE ROSE
The primrose-scented
R. primula *has dainty leaves
and a strikingly simple flower.*

► FIERY FRUITS
The glossy red hips of
Schneezwerg, *a rugosa rose,
provide decorative interest
from late summer to autumn.*

▲ JAGGED EDGE
R. sericea f.
pteracantha *displays
its winged, blood-red
thorns to best
effect in sunlight.*

◄ DOG ROSE
*Commonly seen in
rural hedgerows,*
R. canina *is ideal for
wildflower gardens.*

ORNAMENTAL VALUE

The flowers of wild roses are nearly always single and most flower once only, often early in the season, as with the incense-scented flowers of R. *primula* which appear in late spring. Many of them have a high nectar content, making them very attractive to bees, and possess distinctive scents, like the clove-scented flowers of R. *paulii* or the musk-scented R. *moschata*. In cool, damp conditions and after rain, the leaves of R. *rubiginosa* emit an apple-like fragrance that permeates the air for some distance. This characteristic appears in all its hybrid offspring, the sweet briars, making them a perfect addition to informal hedges or boundary plantings. Some wild roses are among the higher ranks of foliage shrubs: R. *pimpinellifolia* and its offspring boast daintily fern-like leaves and R. *glauca* is admired for its beautiful grey-mauve leaves,

borne on red-purple stems. The many different hips also add to the ornamental value of wild roses and prolong their season of interest. They range from the bristly yellow-green fruits of the chestnut rose, R. *roxburghii*, to the scarlet flasks of R. *moyesii* and the glossy, black hips of the Scots rose, R. *pimpinellifolia*.

GOOD COMBINATIONS

R. glauca *(p.52)* works well with the red-leaved smoke bush, *Cotinus coggygria* 'Royal Purple' and the cream flowers of *Clematis* 'Henryi'. It also looks very effective with the *Clematis* 'Etoile Violette'.

R. x richardii Pink, with the creamy yellow flowers of *Clematis* 'Guernsey Cream'.

R. rubiginosa ✲ *(p.63)* woven in hedging with the fragrant-leaved roses 'Amy Robsart', 'Anne of Geierstein' and 'Lady Penzance', and mid-blue *Clematis alpina* 'Frances Rivis' ✲.

CLIMBERS AND RAMBLERS

WHETHER SCALING WALLS or grown over arches, arbours, pergolas or pillars, climbers and ramblers are invaluable for adding a vertical dimension to your plantings. The difference in their habits makes each of them better suited to certain uses in the garden; climbers are distinguished by their stiff upright growth, which enables them to grow well against walls, while the flexible stems of ramblers make them easier to train over pergolas, pyramids and arches.

ADAPTABLE CLIMBERS

Climbing roses produce large, usually scented blooms, singly or in small clusters. They branch freely to form a rigid, woody framework, bearing flowers on new growth at the stem tips, but mostly on sideshoots from old wood. You can encourage this habit by training stems to the horizontal when still young and flexible. If given their head, climbers bloom freely at the top of the plant, but if the stems are trained sideways or wound around obelisks or pillars, they create walls and towers of scent and colour that last for much

of the summer season. Many climbers are equally useful for clothing unsightly garden structures or for softening the strong lines of formal architectural features. The most vigorous can be grown on pergolas, but they need to be tall-growing if they are to produce sufficient length to clothe the top of the structure. Nearly all climbers are less rampant than ramblers.

Miniature climbers, like 'Laura Ford', rarely exceed 2m and are especially useful in tiny gardens, and can even be grown in containers. Some, like 'Mrs Sam McGredy' or 'Etoile de Hollande', are climbing sports

ROSE TAPESTRY
A reliable and versatile favourite that tolerates poor soils, 'Albertine' is grown here as a sprawling shrub, with clematis scrambling through. It produces clusters of fragrant, soft salmon-pink flowers over many weeks in summer.

STANDING PROUD
'Rosy Mantle' *displays the typical stiffly upright habit of climbing roses. A neat, fragrant rose, it is well suited to training on walls in small gardens.*

ROSE SHOWERS
The long, flexible stems of 'Dorothy Perkins', *bearing dense trusses of double flowers, are typical of rambling roses and are best displayed spilling down from tall structures.*

(mutations caused by a change in their genetic make-up) of large-flowered bush roses. They are often healthier and more vigorous than their parents, and in many cases have overtaken them in popularity.

Climbers are stiffly upright, while ramblers have scrambling stems

ACCOMMODATING HABITS

Ramblers are rampant growers, with long, flexible stems that grow from the base of the plant. They tend to produce many small flowers in often spectacularly large sprays, and most bloom only once, on year-old wood, in early to mid-summer. A few, like 'Sanders' White Rambler' and 'Dorothy Perkins', bloom usefully late in the season when most other once-blooming roses are past their best.

The flexible stems of ramblers are trained easily on to pyramids, pergolas and swags of rope, which all permit free air circulation. Ramblers are a little more prone than climbers to mildew, which thrives in warm, stagnant air; if wall-grown, provide a support that is set away from the wall. The most rampant, like 'Bobbie James' or 'Seagull', are better scrambling through strong, healthy trees to form a cascade of bloom from their branches. When choosing a rose for this purpose, it is essential that you match the vigour of the rose to that of the host tree, as the considerable weight of a mature rambler is quite capable of pulling over a small or weak tree.

GOOD COMBINATIONS

'Albertine' ♥ (rambler) with blue-flowered purple sage, *Salvia officinalis* Purpurascens ♥, and *Linaria* 'Canon Went'.

'Climbing Iceberg' (climber) with *Clematis* 'Marie Boisselot' ♥, both pure white.

'Félicité Perpétue' ♥ (rambler) with *Clematis* 'Huldine', *Fuchsia magellanica* var. *molinae* and *Anemone hupehensis* for a delicate pink and white planting scheme.

'Gloire de Dijon' ♥ (climber), with fragrant, creamy-apricot buff blooms, and *Clematis* 'Polish Spirit', rich purple-blue.

Handel ♥ (climber), cream with magenta-pink petal margins, and the white-flowered *Clematis* 'Duchess of Edinburgh'.

WALLS, PILLARS AND PERGOLAS

To these may also be added arches, arbours, obelisks, tripods, and a whole range of trellis-work as well as existing structures that may need to be brightened with colour or disguised by bushy growth. Whatever the structure, it can be used to provide a focal point in a design or strong vertical elements to a planting scheme. The special training required for roses allows you to display their particular flower forms with impressive effects.

ROSES ON WALLS

Wall-training is nearly always associated with climbers or ramblers, but there are many roses with long flexible stems that enjoy the warmth and thrive best on a wall. Constance Spry, a sprawling, ungainly shrub when free-standing, displays its huge, myrrh-scented soft pink flowers to fabulous effect if trained on a warm-toned wall.

A backdrop of brick or stone can form an attractive foil for rose flowers, but it also has incidental benefits. The reflected warmth of the sun greatly aids the ripening of wood which, in turn, improves the flowering, as ripe wood always flowers more freely. Where the opportunity exists for special training, you are presented with the chance to further increase the flowering potential of a rose. Leading shoots grow relentlessly upwards under the control of hormones which flow back from the topmost bud to suppress branching. If a stem is bent to the horizontal and tied in, the flow of hormones is reduced and sideshoots branch out. In roses, it is these sideshoots that bear most flowers.

ROSE-TRAINED WALL
The soft pink blooms of 'New Dawn' bring out the warmth of a garden wall. This is one of the most shade-tolerant roses and suits a north- or west-facing wall.

◄ PLACE TO PAUSE
A pergola bearing
Compassion
*and 'Aloha' on
its pillars, and
'Sanders' White
Rambler' atop, makes
an attractive focal
point in a garden.*

▼ SOARING PILLAR
*The trunk of an old
apple tree is wreathed
in the sprays of white
flowers produced
by 'Seagull', a
vigorous rambler.*

ADDED DIMENSION

Far from being purely decorative, nearly
all three-dimensional structures permit
good air movement, and so are positively
beneficial to the health of a rose. Again,
special training of roses on these structures
will produce abundant flowers. The stems
of 'Seagull' (*see right*) are wound gently
upwards in a spiral around an old tree
stump to produce a magnificent pillar of
flowers. Similar effects can be achieved
on obelisks or pyramids with climbers,
ramblers or any flexible-stemmed roses.

Winding stems in a gentle upward spiral yields a mass of blooms

For the best results on pergolas, make
sure that you choose a rose that is tall
enough to produce horizontal growth
when it reaches the top of the pillars.
This allows the cascades of flowers to
be appreciated from below. A spectacular
effect is gained by using roses of different
vigour to clothe alternate pillars, with the
most rampant trained to cover the top.

SPECIAL EFFECTS

WHATEVER THE OVERALL STYLE of your plantings, whether they be formal, informal or even wild and naturalistic, some of the most stunning and unexpected effects can be created with roses. It just takes a little special training or some lateral thinking to break free from the idea that roses belong only in beds and borders. With such diversity of habit and form, and a vast catalogue from which to choose, roses offer enormous scope to the adventurous mind.

CASCADES AND COVER

Ground-cover roses with a creeping habit, such as Swany or Pheasant (*see p.60*), display flowers at their best if their stems are allowed to cascade freely. To achieve this, grow them trained as weeping standards (*shown below*), or plant them at the top of a slope or bank, where they will cover the ground, rooting as they go, to create a strong horizontal element.

Ground-cover roses are valued as low-maintenance carpets of bloom. Shrubby types such as Hertfordshire or Flower Carpet (*see p.61*) can create a striking effect where they are used to delineate a garden path and soften its edges, or to provide gradation in height and colour within a rosebed or mixed planting. They are also invaluable for concealing drain covers and other low-level eyesores.

▲ TUMBLING TEARS
The weeping standard form shows trailing ground-cover roses at their best. Here, 'Nozomi' produces a shower of pearl-pink blooms.

▶ FLORAL FANFARE
Low hedges are the forte of ground-cover and patio roses, softening the line of a path, and drawing the eye to the strong focal point of an arch.

GROWING ON A SWAG
A rampant rambler, 'Rambling Rector' *is ideal for training into trees or on ropes as shown here. It bears huge sprays of white flowers in early summer followed by red hips in autumn.*

LENDING HEIGHT AND GRACE

Roses with flexible stems, such as Graham Thomas and Constance Spry (*see p.65*), are among the most versatile of plants when used to add height to a planting scheme. They adapt well to training on vertical structures like pillars and pergolas, but perhaps the most graceful effects are

> ## Flowers cascading from a height create graceful effects

achieved when they are grown to display enormous sprays of flowers cascading from a height. This can be done by training roses, preferably vigorous ramblers, along a rope (or swag) suspended between two posts (*see p.47*); double rows of swags

(catenaries), often with a rose hedge grown beneath, look particularly good either side of a garden path. Training roses into trees or large shrubs also creates a colourful cascade of flowers. It makes an attractive feature of fruit trees, such as apple, as the roses bloom after the tree's flowers are over, extending the season of interest. It is essential that you select a less vigorous rambler, such as 'Blush Rambler' (*see p.69*), that will not overwhelm a small host tree.

GOOD COMBINATIONS

Ferdy, a shrubby ground-cover rose, makes a low hedge at 80cm; it is covered with pale salmon-pink blooms in summer, that will match those of the clove-scented pink, *Dianthus* 'Doris', used as an underplanting.

White Flower Carpet, ground-cover (*p.60*), planted alternately with the purple-flowered lavender 'Hidcote'.

The blue flowers of *Agapanthus* 'Headbourne Hybrids' with **R. Sussex**, a ground-cover rose, forming a 75cm high display of creamy apricot flowers above bronze-green foliage.

'Sanders' White Rambler' (*p.68*) on a swag, matched for vigour with deep purple-flowered *Clematis* 'Jackmanii' on the supporting posts.

CARING FOR YOUR ROSES

BUYING AND PLANTING ROSES

WITH ABOUT 150 SPECIES and thousands of rose hybrids and cultivars available, choosing a rose can be a bewildering task. Make sure that you know what type of rose you are selecting, so that you can be sure that it is suitable for the intended purpose, and you know whether it flowers only once, repeatedly or continuously and, most importantly, how best to prune it.

FINDING THE ROSE YOU WANT

The *Gallery of Roses* (*see pp.53–69*) contains a good selection of all types of rose. The most enjoyable way of finding more is to visit rose gardens in summer, armed with a notebook. Flower colour, form and fragrance will appeal most immediately, but ask advice too, if you need to, on whether the rose blooms once or repeatedly, and whether it is generally healthy. Most garden centres stock a good selection of roses, but if you're unable to find a favourite, refer to *The RHS Plant Finder* or the National Rose Society, which publishes lists of roses and the contact details of reputable mail-order suppliers.

ONE ROSE, TWO NAMES
Many roses have two names. Sweet Dream *is a trade name for* 'Fryminicot', *which is the registered name exclusive to that rose.*

WHAT'S IN A NAME?

Plants are named according to the rules of the International Code of Nomenclature. Names consisting of two words (genus and species) in italics, denote a species, for example *Rosa moyesii*. A species name followed by a name in roman type within inverted commas, for example *R. banksiae* 'Lutea', denotes a cultivar (<u>cult</u>ivated <u>var</u>iety) of a species. An × denotes a simple hybrid that has been cross-bred from two species, e.g. *R.* × *richardii*.

Roses of complex breeding have just one cultivar name in inverted commas, e.g. *R.* 'Agnes'. New introductions are registered by a "code name" to protect the breeder's rights, but may be sold internationally by different trade or selling names (*see above*). Naming rules dictate that the first name registered is the true cultivar name, written in inverted commas. The trade name is written without inverted commas. Both names appear on the plant label.

◀ HEIGHTENED INTEREST *Within a formal potager,* 'White Pet' *makes a striking standard.*

CHOOSING HEALTHY PLANTS

Ideally, all roses offered for sale are well-grown, correctly labelled and healthy but it is always worth running a quick health check on a plant before buying. The soil mix of container-grown roses should be evenly moist and its surface free of mosses and weeds; if choked with weeds, the plant has been in its pot too long and has probably suffered drought or nutrient deficiency. Look for healthy, pale-coloured roots in the compost, and reject plants whose roots are congested, coiled round the pot or protruding from the bottom. Plant carefully to give the rose a good start. An application of mulch after planting (*see p.34*) is recommended.

CHOOSING CONTAINER-GROWN ROSES
The specimen on the left has a well-balanced framework of strong shoots clothed with glossy, dark, disease-free leaves and a complement of flower buds almost ready to open. Avoid buying poor specimens that look like the one shown on the right. The plant has long, spindly stems, and has suffered from leaf drop, probably as a result of drought, disease and nutrient deficiency, as seen in the yellowed leaves that are covered in black spot.

Even covering of flower buds

Leaves show signs of disease

Long, spindly stems with sparse foliage

Glossy, healthy-looking foliage

Moist, firm rootball

GOOD SPECIMEN

POOR SPECIMEN

PLANTING CONTAINER-GROWN BUSH ROSES

Container-grown roses can be planted at any time, provided that the soil is not frozen, sodden or too dry, and that you water well until the rose is established. Dig a planting hole wide enough to hold roots without constriction, and deep enough so that the graft union (a visible "join" low down on the main stem) sits about 2.5cm below the final soil level. Fork half a bucketful of well-rotted organic matter into the hole, with a handful of bonemeal or slow-release fertilizer. Set the rose in and backfill, firming gently as you go. If the plant is in growth, just remove any open flowers; if it's dormant, prune the stems (*right*) for vigorous growth in the spring.

Outward-facing bud will produce open growth

Angled cut made 5mm above bud

PRUNING DORMANT ROSES ON PLANTING
Cut out weak stems to leave 3–5 strong stems. Trim these back, making an angled cut to an outward-facing bud 7–15cm above ground.

BUYING BARE-ROOTED ROSES

Bare-root roses are sold and planted during the dormant season. Look for sturdy roots with a complement of fine fibrous roots, a strong graft union (*see right*), and healthy, well-placed shoots at the top of the plant. Soak the roots in water for an hour before planting. Reject any plants with dried-out roots or sprouting buds, as they won't establish well.

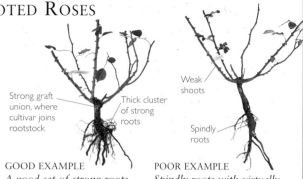

Strong graft union, where cultivar joins rootstock

Thick cluster of strong roots

Weak shoots

Spindly roots

GOOD EXAMPLE
A good set of strong roots and fibrous roots support balanced top growth.

POOR EXAMPLE
Spindly roots with virtually no system of fibrous roots result in poor top growth.

PLANTING BARE-ROOTED ROSES

1 **Prune the top growth** using clean, sharp secateurs, to remove any weak, crossing, damaged or dead shoots. Trim back any roots that are damaged to clean, healthy live roots.

2 **Dig a hole** wide enough to hold the roots unrestricted and deep enough for the graft union to be 2.5cm below the soil level. Fork well-rotted organic matter into the bottom.

3 **Insert the rose** and check the depth by placing a cane across the hole; the graft union needs to be 2.5cm below the cane.

4 **Backfill gently,** making sure roots are in close contact with the soil by firming in as you go. Water in and prune (*see facing page*).

PLANTING AND STAKING STANDARDS

A standard rose is formed by grafting a bush rose (or trailing rose if it is a weeping standard) on to the top of a long straight stem trained from a vigorous rootstock. The head should have an evenly spaced and well-balanced set of strong shoots growing from a strong graft union. You can usually prune to correct an unbalanced head, but only consider buying a poor specimen if you get a worthwhile discount on the selling price. The straight stem and union always prove to be the weakest points on a standard rose, and so it will need the support of a sturdy stake – one that is long enough to reach the graft union – throughout its life.

1 Dig a planting hole as for bare-root roses. Drive in a stake to a depth of about 45cm. Place the rose in the hole, checking the depth by placing a cane across the top. The final soil level should be the same as it was before; use the old soil mark on the stem as a guide.

2 The top of the stake should reach the graft union and the stake should be on the side of the prevailing wind. This prevents the plant from leaning into the stake, which would cause chafing of the bark and possibly breakage of the entire head in strong winds.

3 Attach the rose to the stake using rose ties with rubber buffers between stem and stake. Put one at the top to support the head and one half-way up the stem. Check they are not too tight, and allow some room for expansion. Cut out weak or crossing shoots.

PLANTING AND TRAINING CLIMBING ROSES

When planting climbers, it is important that you don't cut them back hard as you do with bush roses. Many are climbing sports (mutations) of bush roses and if pruned too hard, they may revert to a bush habit. In contrast, ramblers naturally produce strong shoots from low down and so need hard pruning on planting. When hard-pruned they produce strong new shoots which can be tied in to the support. Plant both climbers and ramblers about 45cm away from their wall or support; this avoids the very dry soil usually found at the base of walls. The shoots can then be guided to the base of the support with ties and canes, which can be removed later.

Position at angle to avoid dry soil at base of wall

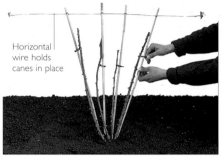

Horizontal wire holds canes in place

1 **For climbers and ramblers,** the hole should hold the roots easily when stems are set at an angle of 45°. Check the depth with a cane to make sure that the final level is the same as the old soil marks on the stems.

2 **Spread out** 4 or 5 of the strongest stems and tie them to canes pushed into the soil at the base and attached to the lowest wires. Use clips or soft twine for tying in, but check all ties regularly to avoid stem constriction.

WALL-TRAINING AND PRUNING
A CLIMBER IN ITS FIRST SUMMER
The aims of early training are to achieve good coverage by fanning the shoots out so that flowers appear from top to bottom.

3 **Tip-prune** strong unbranched shoots to encourage sideways-branching sideshoots.

1 **Tie in** new growth to build a framework, training shoots so they will grow sideways; tie them to wires as they extend.

2 **Cut out** any spindly, dead or damaged shoots. Remove original canes and ties.

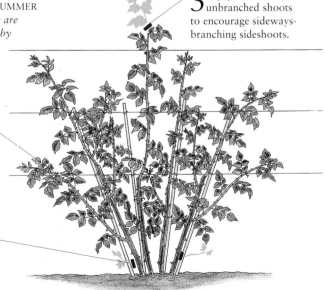

ROUTINE CARE

Roses use up considerable energy in producing flowers and replacing growth removed by pruning – that's why they are referred to as "hungry" plants. If you want your roses to grow well and reward you with good-quality flowers all summer long, you need to keep them well fed and healthy. And before you plant, bear in mind that new roses seldom thrive in soils where roses have grown before; they usually succumb to rose sickness (*see p.48*).

FEEDING, WATERING AND MULCHING

A fertile, well-cultivated, weed-free soil is the key to healthy and productive roses. Ideally, prepare it well about three months before planting. Roses prefer a slightly acid, moist but well-drained soil, at about pH 6.5. You can lower the pH of acid soils by adding lime and raise that of alkaline soils with organic matter. Rotted farmyard manure or garden compost can be used to improve nutrient retention, drainage and soil moisture. After spring pruning, feed with a proprietary rose fertilizer at the recommended rate and mulch with an 8cm layer of organic matter to retain moisture

THIRSTY AT FIRST
Water roses regularly until they are fully established; thereafter, they will only need water during prolonged spells of dry weather.

and suppress weeds. Fertilizer given after mid-summer induces soft growth which is prone to frost damage. Instead, use a high-potash feed (75g/sq m) in early autumn to help ripen wood.

LOOKING AFTER ROSES IN CONTAINERS

Patio and miniature roses are ideal for growing in containers, but their restricted root run means that they rely heavily on regular watering and feeding. Choose a pot that is 30–45cm in depth for patio roses or 23–35cm for miniature roses. Before planting up, place a piece of mesh over the drainage hole in the bottom and cover with broken crocks. Raise the pot above the ground, using "feet" for example. Fill with a good-quality, loam-based potting compost, as this gives weight for stability, retains nutrients and is less susceptible to drying out than a peat-based equivalent. Plant the rose in the same way and at the same depth as roses in open ground, but leave about 3cm between the soil surface and pot rim to allow for watering. Top-dress with balanced fertilizer after pruning in spring and give a foliar or liquid feed in the growing season – but don't feed later than mid-summer. Check the plant daily for ailments and water thoroughly if the compost is dry.

Leaves sprayed with foliar feed in growing season

Compost surface 3cm below rim allows for watering

CONTAINER ROSE

REMOVING ROSE SUCKERS

Most roses are bud-grafted on to specially selected rootstock belonging to a different, usually more vigorous, species. This means that when shoots or "suckers" grow from the roots, they are likely to be stronger than those of the grafted cultivar, and may eventually become dominant if they are not removed promptly. Suckers usually arise some distance from the base of the rose and can be clearly identified by their leaf form and colour which differ markedly from that of the grafted rose. Before you remove a sucker, protect your hands with stout, thornproof gloves so that you can grasp it firmly, and make sure that you trace the sucker right back to its point of origin, scraping soil gently away from the roots to do so. Cutting off the sucker at ground level often leaves it with dormant buds that will be stimulated into growth.

1 **Trace the sucker** back to its point of origin on the stem base or root below the graft union, and scrape away the soil carefully by hand or with a trowel.

2 **Grasp the sucker** firmly and pull it away with a sharp and determined tug; this may not be as easy as cutting, but it is far less likely to result in sucker regrowth.

TYING IN CLIMBING AND RAMBLING ROSES

In the wild, roses are held in place by their hooked thorns as they scramble through host plants. When grown on more formal supports, however, climbers and ramblers need to be tied in regularly as their growth extends. When tying on to wires, use rose ties or soft twine in a figure-of-eight configuration; this is loose enough to allow the stems to expand and buffers them against rubbing or chafing by the wires. On tripods, attach a series of horizontal wires and tie in stems at intervals so that they grow in a spiral fashion around the support. On swags (ropes), guide stems around the rope while they are still young and flexible and secure them at regular intervals with soft twine.

TYING ON TO WIRE   TYING TO A TRIPOD

GUIDING SHOOTS ALONG A ROPE SWAG

ROUTINE PRUNING

R OSES MAY NEED PRUNING for health at any time (*see facing page*) and all types benefit from annual or seasonal pruning to a greater or lesser degree (*see pp.38–45*). Always make clean, correct cuts (*see below*) and use the right tool for the job; use secateurs for shoots of 1cm or less in diameter; loppers for shoots up to about 2.5cm across; and a pruning saw for anything bigger.

CUTTING ROSE STEMS

To achieve the ideal cut, aim to make an incision about 5mm above a bud, angled slightly with the lowest end of the cut just opposite the bud, so that rain is shed away from the bud rather than onto it.

The narrow blade of your secateurs is the cutting blade, so keep this edge nearest to the bud to which you are cutting; otherwise, you crush the stem, leaving a jagged injury that is open to infection.

CUTTING CLEANLY
The correct way to make a cut applies to removing dead wood, deadheading, and all annual pruning. Cuts must be clean, so keep your secateurs sharp. If you happen to snag a stem or make the cut too close to the bud, cut back the shoot to the next sound, healthy bud.

Correctly angled cut 5mm above a bud

CORRECT CUT

Bruised tissue is slow to heal

ROUGH CUT

Cut slopes towards not away from bud

BADLY ANGLED

Too high above the bud

TOO HIGH

DAMAGING CUTS
A rough cut that crushes the stem allows infection to enter; a badly angled cut sheds rain onto the new bud, and too high a cut leads to stem dieback from the stub.

Narrow cutting blade next to bud

Healthy bud in leaf axil

CUTTING WITH SECATEURS
Always make cuts to a healthy bud facing in the desired direction of growth. Use secateurs for stems of 1cm or less; thicker stems strain the tool and will be bruised or crushed.

Stem fits into lopper's bite without straining

USING LOPPERS
Choose loppers to cut large stems; make sure that the stem fits comfortably within the bite of the loppers without straining. For extra leverage, use a pair with long handles.

REMOVING DEAD, DISEASED AND DAMAGED STEMS

Cut out dead, diseased and damaged stems as soon as you notice them throughout the growing season as well as during pruning in the dormant season. Although the best time to remove crossing shoots is in the dormant season, if they rub and chafe other stems they will cause the sort of damage that allows disease-bearing organisms easy access. Since small, clean cuts heal more rapidly than chafing wounds, it is safer to remedy crossing stems in the growing season, by cutting to a bud that is facing in a better direction.

With roses, wood that has been dead for some time is usually isolated by the plant's own natural protective barriers, leaving a clear demarcation line between living and dead tissue. Where possible, always make a cut just above the living wood, otherwise cut to a healthy bud or shoot. Sometimes, however, stem death is caused by a progressive condition known as dieback, which travels back down the stem, staining the inner tissue brown.

White pith indicates healthy wood

REMOVING DIEBACK
Light brown, dried-up stems with no clear line between live and dead tissue probably indicate dieback. To remove the disease, pruning cuts need to be made below the affected portion, so keep cutting back as far as necessary to buds further down the stem until you reach healthy white pith.

HOW TO DEADHEAD ROSES

Deadheading roses on a warm, dry evening in summer is one of the most therapeutic of tasks, but if it is to benefit the rose as much as the pruner it must be done correctly. The three main purposes are to improve appearances, to prevent the plant using up its energy in setting seed, and in repeat-flowering roses, to encourage further flushes of good-quality flowers. Never remove just the flowered head, but cut back to a full-size leaf that is two or three buds further down the stem.

CLUSTER-FLOWERED ROSES
Prune out the entire cluster of flowers, making a correctly angled cut to a healthy bud further down the stem. You can pinch out the central flower that fades first.

LARGE- AND SINGLE-FLOWERED ROSES
Cut the faded flower back to a healthy bud or sideshoot that is further down the stem, to encourage the production of more flowering shoots later in the season.

PRUNING MODERN BUSH ROSES

THE MODERN BUSH ROSES include large- and cluster-flowered roses as well as their smaller counterparts, patio, miniature and ground-cover roses, which have relatively minimal pruning needs. Nearly all of the roses in these groups are repeat-flowering, with some of them blooming almost continuously during summer and well into autumn. They bloom most freely on young stems and, with the exception of ground-covering roses, they are best pruned annually in the dormant season to prevent the base of the bush from becoming bare and to create a strong, low framework from which sturdy flowering shoots arise.

PRUNING LARGE-FLOWERED BUSH ROSES

Large-flowered bush roses should be pruned hard on planting or in their first dormant season (*see p.30*) to within 7–15cm of ground level. Cut back strong shoots to an outward-facing bud, so that new shoots grow out evenly around an open centre. During the growing season, remove diseased, dead, damaged and crossing shoots, cut out suckers, and deadhead faded flowers, as necessary

(*see p.37*). When pruning in the dormant season, cut out all unproductive and unhealthy growth and shorten stems to recreate an open, shapely bush. This stops the bush becoming bare, resulting in few flowers at the tips of leggy stems. It also helps to prevent the build-up of dead wood and keeps an open centre through which light and air can penetrate freely, thus reducing the risk of fungal diseases.

LARGE-FLOWERED BUSH ROSE
Prune when dormant between autumn and early spring. In cold climates, delay until spring, as late as possible, to avoid frost damage to soft new shoots.

1 Remove spindly shoots of less than pencil thickness; they don't flower well and are prone to disease.

2 Cut back dead, diseased or damaged shoots to strong buds or healthy wood.

3 Shorten all strong stems to about 20–22cm above ground level, to let in light and air. Use an angled cut made above an outward-facing bud.

PRUNING FOR WINTER PROTECTION

Where winters are cold, delay pruning dormant roses until spring. However, any long shoots remaining on the bush during winter may cause wind resistance, increasing slightly the risk of damage or infection from disease. The rocking motion caused by wind also loosens roots and creates a gap between roots and soil at ground level. If water enters the gap and freezes it can cause irreparable damage to the graft union – the most vulnerable part of the plant. To prevent this, shorten all shoots by one-third to half of their length in autumn. After frosts and strong winds, check the bush and refirm the soil at the base if necessary.

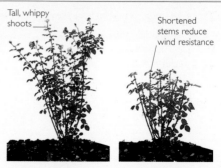

Tall, whippy shoots

Shortened stems reduce wind resistance

BEFORE PRUNING   AFTER PRUNING

PRUNING CLUSTER-FLOWERED BUSH ROSES

Cluster-flowered bushes are pruned in the same way and at the same time as large-flowered bushes, but not so hard. The effect of massed clusters of small flowers is the greatest part of their charm, so aim to keep long lengths of shoot bearing plenty of buds; from each bud a potential flowering shoot grows. When deadheading large trusses of flowers from cluster-flowered roses, it is sometimes difficult to find a suitable bud to which to cut. In this case, cut back to the desired height; this usually stimulates a dormant bud into life, and any stubs can be cut away later.

CLUSTER-FLOWERED BUSH ROSE
Prune hard on planting or in their first dormant season, as for large-flowered bush roses, to outward-facing buds 7–15cm above ground level. When the rose is established, prune less severely to ensure a long succession of flowers.

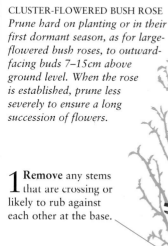

3 Keep the bush open by cutting back the remaining stems to 25–30cm above ground level.

1 Remove any stems that are crossing or likely to rub against each other at the base.

2 Cut back all dead, diseased and damaged shoots to the base.

4 Shorten any sideshoots (laterals) to two or three buds from the main stem, making the cut to an outward-facing bud.

PRUNING PATIO AND MINIATURE ROSES

Patio roses are essentially dwarf versions of cluster-flowered roses, so the timing and technique of pruning is the same as for their larger counterparts – but not so hard. Deadhead them during summer and prune annually when dormant. The miniatures, mostly tiny counterparts of large- and cluster-flowered bushes, should be pruned hard on planting, to 5–8cm above soil level. If they are growing and flowering well, they need only light pruning. If you notice, though, that the rose is not growing well, prune it hard. Remove all but the strongest stems and shorten these drastically by two-thirds.

MINIATURE ROSES
Precise prescriptions as to the height of cut are difficult, as bush size varies; as a rule, reducing the bush by about one-third will be satisfactory.

2 **Tip-prune** the main stems, making sure that you also remove the last of the season's faded flowers.

1 **Cut out** the oldest stems entirely on congested bushes, and remove dead, diseased, damaged and crossing wood.

3 **Prune back** any sideshoots to within two or three buds of a main stem, to reduce congestion and to stimulate flower bud production for next year.

PRUNING GROUND-COVER ROSES

Shrubby ground-cover roses need only routine removal of dead wood and deadheading. A little tip-pruning of overlong stems and shortening of laterals may be needed to open up the centre of the bush. For rambler types, peg down or cut back overlong stems (*below and right*) depending on how much room is available.

Second-year stems become prostrate under the weight of flowering shoots

Flexible, first-year stems can be pegged down

PEGGING DOWN
The flexible, rooting stems of rambler-type ground-cover roses can be pegged down to increase flowering potential and extend cover.

LONG, RAMBLER-TYPE STEMS
Little pruning is necessary, other than to keep the plant within bounds; cut back overlong shoots to an upward-facing bud or shoot.

PRUNING STANDARDS

The aim of pruning a standard rose is to produce a balanced, open head on a clear stem. The height of the stem will vary, from 50cm for patios and miniatures, 75cm for half-standards, to 1.1m for full standards; weeping standards are the tallest of all (1.5–2m). For each type, prune the head according to the group of rose grafted on the top of the stem; try to imagine that you are pruning, for example, a large- or cluster-flowered rose and pretend that the graft union is at ground level. Prune repeat-flowering roses in the dormant season; once-flowering roses after flowering.

Pinch shoot between thumb and forefinger

SUCKERS ON STANDARD STEMS
Throughout the growing season, check for and remove any suckers that appear on the clear stem by pinching them out.

BEFORE PRUNING
The framework has been shortened in autumn to prevent winter damage. When danger of frost has passed, prune to restore a balanced head and to encourage new flowering growth.

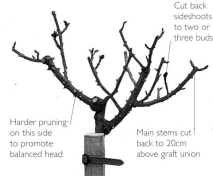

Cut back sideshoots to two or three buds

Harder pruning on this side to promote balanced head

Main stems cut back to 20cm above graft union

AFTER PRUNING
Dead, crossing and unproductive old wood has been removed. Remaining stems are shortened to about 20cm from the graft union, and laterals shortened to 2–3 buds.

TRIMMING WEEPING STANDARDS

Weeping standards may be created using ramblers, lax climbers or trailing ground-cover roses. Do not prune them for the first couple of years, but remove any dead, diseased or damaged shoots and shorten spindly shoots to strong buds. Once they are established, they can be pruned according to the rose type. Vigorous ramblers often produce so many new stems that all flowered shoots can be removed each year, cutting back to new basal shoots. On less vigorous ones, prune back one in three of the flowered shoots each year, cutting to upward- or outward-facing buds.

SHORTENING STEMS

REMOVING OLD STEMS

PRUNING SHRUB ROSES

THE SHRUB ROSES include the species, old garden roses and modern shrubs and, unlike modern bush roses, most flower on old wood. They are best allowed to develop their full grace and stature with light annual pruning to keep them shapely and to maintain a balance between old wood and vigorous new growth. Exact requirements depend on the growth and flowering habit of an individual cultivar, but in general, those that flower once in mid-summer are pruned after flowering, while those that repeat are pruned when dormant.

PRUNING OLD GARDEN ROSES

Old roses are pruned lightly on planting; tip-prune any overlong stems and remove damaged or dead shoots. Established roses are pruned in one of two ways (*see box, opposite*): treat those with dense habits like Gallicas (*below*), removing one or two of the oldest stems each year and shortening back the sideshoots close to a main stem to reduce congestion. Others are pruned like Albas, which have more spreading growth.

ESTABLISHED GALLICA ROSE
After flowering, prune to reduce crowding and cut out all dead, diseased, damaged and crossing shoots. In autumn, long whippy stems that extend beyond the main outline can be shortened so that they are not damaged by winter winds.

3 Shorten sideshoots by about one-third of their length, cutting back to a strong, healthy, outward-facing bud.

2 Keep the rose healthy by removing all dead, damaged or weak stems, as well as any rubbing against another stem.

1 Cut out one or two old, woody stems at the base.

THE DIFFERENT SHRUB ROSE GROUPS

• Alba roses are treated in a similar way to Gallicas (*see left, below*), but because they are less dense, you rarely need to cut out entire main stems. Prune after flowering by reducing main shoots to one-third of their length and sideshoots by about two-thirds. Shorten any overlong stems by about one-third in autumn (*see p.39*), cutting to upward-growing shoots.

• Damask, Centifolia and Moss roses are all pruned in the same way as Alba roses. Hedge plants can be trimmed lightly in winter, but don't attempt to shape them formally.

• Bourbon, China and Portland roses are treated like Albas, but they are repeat-flowering, so pruning is done during the dormant season.

• Hybrid musks are vigorous leafy shrubs that flower repeatedly in summer. In the dormant season, take out one in three of the oldest, unproductive stems, shorten the remainder by up to one-third, then shorten laterals by half.

• Rugosa roses are repeat-flowering and also bear ornamental hips. Prune them during winter, by tipping back long stems and taking out old stems occasionally.

PRUNING MODERN SHRUB ROSES

Many modern shrubs can be pruned lightly as shown here; some are large versions of cluster-flowered bush roses and are pruned similarly (*see p.39*), reducing main stems by one-third and laterals by two-thirds for a compact habit and more flower buds.

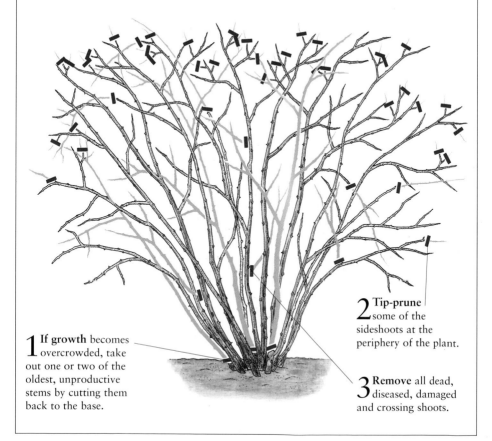

2 Tip-prune some of the sideshoots at the periphery of the plant.

1 If growth becomes overcrowded, take out one or two of the oldest, unproductive stems by cutting them back to the base.

3 Remove all dead, diseased, damaged and crossing shoots.

PRUNING CLIMBERS AND RAMBLERS

CLIMBERS AND RAMBLERS can be trained in a variety of ways, but are most often grown on vertical walls or fences. Here, they need the strong support of horizontal wires, set at least 5cm away from the vertical surface to let air circulate freely. Careful training that permits relatively easy access to all parts of the rose will make it much easier to release and adjust ties when pruning, especially when removing entire main stems – this is occasionally necessary for climbers but a regular requirement when pruning ramblers.

PRUNING CLIMBING ROSES

Climbers are mainly repeat-flowering and are pruned when dormant. Don't prune them hard on planting; just remove dead or damaged wood and weak, spindly shoots. If, once growth begins, the plant is slow to branch, tip-prune main stems by about 5–8cm, cutting to a strong bud; this will stimulate laterals to break. Fan out main stems, as nearly horizontal as you can, and tie them in at even spacings as they grow. Aim to cover the lower parts of the wall well; gaps will be difficult to fill later on.

PRUNING AN
ESTABLISHED CLIMBER
If possible, prune early in dormancy, in autumn, to reduce the risk of long stems being whipped about in winter winds. Walls give more protection than is afforded to plants in the open, so there's less need to delay pruning till spring.

1 **Prune** flowered shoots by two-thirds of their length, making angled cuts just above a healthy shoot or bud.

2 **Check ties** and loosen any that constrict stems. Reposition or shorten any shoots that cross or rub against each other.

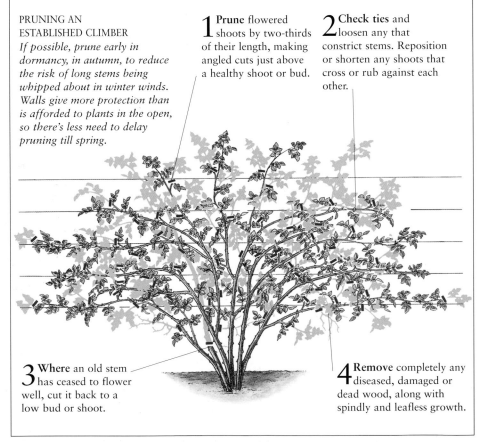

3 **Where** an old stem has ceased to flower well, cut it back to a low bud or shoot.

4 **Remove** completely any diseased, damaged or dead wood, along with spindly and leafless growth.

PRUNING RAMBLERS

Ramblers produce new stems from their base each year and flower most freely on wood grown in the previous season, so the techniques and timing for pruning differ from those used for climbers. Ramblers usually flower once in summer and are pruned just after flowering. Prune them hard on planting to about 40cm above ground level to encourage strong shoots. The stems are flexible, so fanning them out to the horizontal to cover an allotted space is easier than it is for climbers. When routinely pruning an established plant, aim to take out about one in three old flowered stems, to encourage replacement shoots. If you wish, you can cut back all flowered stems but this reduces the plant's stature and, in any case, plants flower perfectly well on the same wood for several years.

OUT-OF-REACH ROSES

Left to their own devices, climbers and ramblers grow steadily upwards towards maximum sunlight, producing flowers only at the top of the stems. If you train and prune correctly from the start, the problem is avoided. But if you inherit a neglected specimen, it may be brought back into production by drastic renovation. For ramblers, you can either cut all stems down to the base and wait a season for flowers, or you can cut out old, moribund stems and leave 3–4 young ones, cutting their sideshoots back by 8–10cm. For climbers, cut a proportion of the main stems (1 in 3) back to within 30cm of ground level. If the plant is capable of doing so, it produces new stems low down that can be tied in to the support. Some cultivars are reluctant to respond and for these, disguising bare bases with other plants is probably your best option.

PRUNING A RAMBLER
The main aim when pruning established ramblers is to ensure regular replacement of old flowered shoots with new ones that will flower more freely.

1 Cut back one in three of the oldest flowered stems to ground level; remove them in sections to avoid tearing the bark of remaining stems.

2 Shorten sideshoots from remaining stems by about two-thirds, to encourage them to form flowering shoots.

3 Tip-prune the main stems by 5–8cm, to encourage them to produce flowering sideshoots and to confine them to bounds.

4 Check ties during the growing season and loosen any that constrict stems. Tie in new stems regularly using a figure-of-eight tie to allow for stem expansion.

SPECIAL TRAINING FOR ROSES

SOME OF THE most effective forms of special training are produced on vertical features, like tripods and obelisks. The key to success here depends on applying the principle of training stems to the horizontal. This encourages flowering sideshoots to grow out evenly all along the length of the stems rather than in a cluster at the top of the structure, as they would if left to their own devices. For the best results, use roses with flexible stems.

TRAINING ROSES ON A TRIPOD

Plant a flexible-stemmed rose about 25cm from the base of each of the tripod legs. Climbers and shrub roses need pruning on planting; cut back ramblers to about 40cm above ground to stimulate strong new shoots. Tie in the stems as they grow, winding them in a spiral fashion around the support to as near horizontal as possible. You will find subsequent pruning easier if you can arrange the stems parallel to each other; any formality will be disguised by leaf growth.

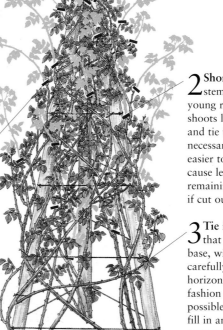

PRUNING A TRIPOD ROSE
For established climbers, maintain a permanent framework of main stems and in autumn, cut back flowered sideshoots to an outward-facing bud. For established ramblers, after flowering, cut back flowered sideshoots by two-thirds and tip-prune main stems. Remove one or two main stems each year.

1 **Cut back** flowered shoots and any new long shoots not needed for tying in, to maintain the tripod's outline.

2 **Shorten** some older stems to strong young replacement shoots low down, and tie these in where necessary. Old stems are easier to remove, and cause least damage to remaining shoots, if cut out in sections.

3 **Tie in** new stems that grow from the base, winding them carefully towards the horizontal, in spiral fashion and, where possible, use them to fill in any low-down gaps as you go.

PRUNING ROSE SWAGS

For swags and catenaries (swags in double rows), you need strong, upright pillars 2–2.5m tall, and a length of stout ship's rope, about 1.2–1.5m longer than the distance between the posts. This allows for a 60cm dip between them, and brings blooms to eye level. Plant one rose 30cm from the base of each post. Train them straight up the post and then along the rope. On single swags, train the roses to meet mid-way; for catenaries, train all the roses in the same direction except the one on the last post, where the shoots are trained to meet the preceding rose. Each year, prune out flowered stems and tie in new growth to maintain the shape (*below*).

1 **Before pruning,** identify any vigorous new shoots that have grown upwards, spoiling the line of the swag. If these shoots are tied down without removing other stems, growth quickly becomes overcongested.

2 **Wearing stout gloves** and safety goggles to protect you against thorns, carefully detach rose stems from the rope and unwind them so that each stem and its sideshoots can be clearly distinguished from the others.

3 **Prune back each** of the flowered main stems to a strong, new shoot. Aim to create an L-shape in the direction of growth. Stems growing in the same direction as the rope will be much easier to tie in.

4 **Taking care** not to damage growth at the junction between the sideshoots and the main stem, gently straighten the L-shaped stems and wind them around the rope, tying them at intervals with soft twine in a figure-of-eight.

KEEPING ROSES HEALTHY

ONE OF THE MOST IMPORTANT ways of ensuring that you have healthy roses is to take good care of the soil in which they grow. Keep the soil well aerated, moisture-retentive but well-drained and adequately fertile by mulching annually with well-rotted organic matter, and by applying fertilizer in spring and after the first flush of flowers. This will help your roses to grow strongly, to be more resistant to diseases and to recover quickly from any pest infestations. Correct pruning to permit good air flow and access of light to all parts, and the removal of damaged, diseased or dead wood as well as faded blooms to conserve the plant's energy, will put you on the path to success.

AVOIDING PROBLEMS

When you visit rose gardens, you will notice that some roses are more healthy than others, even though they have been raised in identical growing conditions. Some roses, including the Albas, the Rugosas, most climbers and many modern shrubs are, quite simply, more disease-resistant than others. Choosing notably healthy roses is your first line of defence. The second is to maintain good hygiene. Always remove and burn diseased material immediately, including any fallen infected leaves that harbour fungal spores. Bear in mind that good air circulation is anathema to many fungal infections. The third is to create conditions that deter the proliferation of pests and diseases. You can stem population growth of insect pests by encouraging beneficial insects in your garden; ladybirds, hoverflies and predatory wasps consume aphids. Before you reach for the spray gun, make every effort to distinguish between friend and foe.

LADYBIRD

BLIND SHOOTS
Non-flowering shoots often grow from frosted shoot tips. Prune back to a bud in the axil of a healthy leaf for a new flowering shoot.

Shoot with no terminal flower bud

Bud concealed in leaf axil

DISEASE-RESISTANT ROSES

Alexander	Northamptonshire
Anna Ford	'Nozomi' ♥
Escapade ♥ *(cluster-flowered, rose-violet)*	Princess Alice
Flower Carpet ♥	Rose Gaujard *(large-flowered, carmine-red, paler reverse)*
Francine Austin *(cluster-flowered, pure white)*	Sheila's Perfume
Freedom ♥	Suma ♥ *(ground cover, deep pink)*
Hertfordshire	Sweet Dream ♥
Indian Summer	Tequila Sunrise ♥
Ingrid Bergman ♥	'The Fairy' ♥
Just Joey	The Lady ♥ *(large-flowered, yellow)*
Kent	
Little Bo-peep	'The Queen Elizabeth' ♥
Lovely Lady ♥	The Times Rose ♥
Mary Rose	

DAMAGE LIMITATION

It is almost inevitable – in some seasons more so than others – that roses attract one or other of the most common problems (*see below*). Damage limitation relies on rapid action; if you treat as soon as seen, you reduce the risk of pest proliferation and avoid the spread of diseases, which attack soft tissues first. If you do lose roses to disease, weeding will remove any "reservoirs" of infection and help to avert rose sickness, where new plantings fail to thrive for no obvious reason – affected roses may recover if replanted elsewhere. Always weed by hand around the root zone of roses to avoid incurring any damage to fragile feeder roots.

USING SPRAYS

If used appropriately, most chemical sprays present few problems to the environment and are certainly effective in controlling pests and diseases, but always assess whether the problem really justifies their use. Any slight infestations may be dealt with by nipping off affected parts, or even by squashing pests by hand. If possible, use a pest-specific chemical, like pirimicarb, which kills only aphids. The use of a combined insecticide and fungicide is only justifiable when both problems are present at levels that warrant control. Having made sure that the chemical suits the purpose, always follow the manufacturers' instructions as to timing, application rate and frequency of use. Applications are best made at dusk, when most beneficial insects have stopped flying.

APHIDS
Present from mid-spring onwards. Treat before heavy infestation develops; pick off or use pirimicarb.

SAWFLY DAMAGE
Rolled leaflets in late spring to early summer; harmless but ugly. Pick off light infestations or use systemic insecticide.

BLACK SPOT
Purple-black spots, yellowing and leaf drop; use systemic fungicide after spring pruning; repeat as advised on the label.

POWDERY MILDEW
Cut out and burn any leaves with powdery white bloom; use systemic fungicide. Keep well mulched and watered.

ROSE LEAFHOPPERS
Leaf speckling in summer; tiny, pale yellow, sap-sucking insects beneath. Control with a systemic insecticide.

ROSE BALLING
Prevalent in wet weather; not immediately harmful, but prune out before blooms go mouldy and admit dieback.

DISPLAYING ROSES

ROSES MAKE LOVELY CUT FLOWERS, and a little care *(see below)* helps to prolong their beauty. Showing your roses can be a most satisfying, although challenging and very competitive activity. Standards of cultivation are impeccable at shows, and rules for exhibiting are detailed and strict. If you are bitten by the bug and have the time to devote to growing for exhibition, your first step should be to join your local or national rose society where you can enjoy access to a wealth of knowledge and experience.

SHOWING TECHNIQUES

Exhibition roses are usually shown in groups of three or more to permit selection of the perfect bloom. Plants are pruned to a limited number of shoots and fed heavily to yield only 8–9 flowers per year; flowers are disbudded to produce quality blooms. There are also precise rules to which you need to conform when staging roses; for example, a large-flowered bloom must be three-quarters open at judging, while cluster-flowered roses have blooms in a cycle of openness, but without any fading of the stamens. Even when you have the perfect blooms, you must conform to show schedules to avoid disqualification.

DISBUDDING LARGE-FLOWERED ROSES
Pinch out newly formed sidebuds so that the main bud develops strongly.

DISBUDDING CLUSTER-FLOWERED ROSES
Pinch out the central bud of a cluster so other blooms open at the same time.

CARING FOR CUT FLOWERS

Nearly all roses are suitable for cutting, but they usually need the support of florists' foam or a scrunch of wire netting. Cut roses early in the day when the blooms are about three-quarters open – try to cut about 30cm of stem. Remove thorns and some of the lower leaves, then plunge them to their necks in cold, fresh water for a few hours before arranging. Cut roses last longer if you make a slanting cut across the stems while still submerged. Use a proprietary cut flower food and change the water every two or three days. In arrangements, roses mix well with the formal spires of delphiniums and airy panicles of gypsophila, or with cornflower or larkspur. For foliage contrast, use silver artemisia, ferns or dark-leaved cotinus.

WILD BEAUTY
Even species roses can be used as cut flowers; they are especially effective in naturalistic arrangements. For foliage interest, use the ferny-leaved R. pimpinellifolia, the grey-leaved R. glauca or R. rugosa (above).

A CALENDAR OF ROSE CARE

SPRING

- Plant new container-grown roses and complete plantings of bare-root roses. Heel in bare-root roses and keep container-grown ones well-watered if planting is delayed. Soak well before and after planting.
- Prune newly planted modern bush and standard roses, and other repeat-flowering roses, in early spring.
- When soil is thoroughly moist, apply fertilizer to the base of established plants and water it in; mulch with well-rotted organic matter.
- Repot roses grown in containers and apply a top dressing of rose fertilizer.
- Start checking for pest and disease infestations (see p.49) and treat immediately.
- Check for and remove suckers.

SUMMER

- Plant newly acquired container-grown roses, but not in prolonged spells of dry weather. Water until well established.
- Thin Gallicas, and prune once-flowering roses after flowering.
- Deadhead repeat-flowering roses and others not grown for ornamental hips; give a second application of fertilizer after the first flush of flowers.
- Water established, open-ground roses in prolonged drought, and roses in pots each or every other day, as necessary.
- Maintain weed control throughout the growing season.
- Check regularly and treat pests and diseases, if necessary, as soon as seen.
- Train and tie in strong new shoots of climbers throughout the growing season.
- Peruse mail-order catalogues and order for new plantings in autumn and winter.

AUTUMN

- Prepare soil for new plantings; cultivate deeply and incorporate well-rotted organic matter.
- Shorten long shoots of climbers and begin pruning bush roses in mild-winter regions.
- Trim back long stems on bush and shrub roses to reduce wind rock in winter.
- Trim roses grown as informal hedging; delay pruning plants with a display of hips until late winter.
- Begin planting bare-root roses in spells of fine weather if soil is moist and workable. If weather is poor, heel them in and keep roots moist until conditions improve.
- Cut back any summer-flowering companion perennials; divide and replant if necessary.
- Collect and burn dead wood, fallen leaves, and other debris, especially that affected by disease.

WINTER

- Continue to plant in spells of mild weather when soil is not wet or frozen. If planting of container-grown roses is delayed, protect pot and roots from frosts.
- Move any young roses that you have sited badly, but do not replant in soil that roses have grown in before.
- Check regularly for soil heave after frosts and high winds, and refirm soil around the roots if necessary.
- In cold winters, mound soil over crowns; in very harsh winters, use a deep, dry mulch of straw or bracken, held in place with netting or similar. In extreme conditions, lift and bury roses on their sides in a deep, straw-lined trench and cover with 30cm of soil.
- Renovate old, neglected roses of all types.

HOLIDAY WATERING
A full bucket of water with a "wick" of fabric pushed into the compost gives roses in pots access to water while you are away.

MOUNDING SOIL
In areas where winter temperatures are likely to fall below -10°C, mound soil over the crown of each rose plant to a minimum depth of 12cm in late autumn. This protects the vulnerable graft union from becoming frozen.

A GALLERY OF ROSES

THE ROSES DESCRIBED HERE are grouped according to a system of classification that is recognized by rose societies worldwide. Roses are grouped by flower form, size and habit and all those selected have a good health record and are fully hardy. The symbol ♡ denotes the RHS Award of Garden Merit.

LARGE-FLOWERED BUSH ROSES

Pristine
Scented, high-pointed flowers with a pink flush. To 1.2m.

ALSO KNOWN AS HYBRID TEAS, these have a bushy or upright habit, and bear large, usually many-petalled, and often fragrant flowers, singly or in clusters of three. Most flower throughout summer to autumn, either continuously or in successive flushes. They are traditionally pruned hard every year (*see p.38*) for the finest flowers; regular deadheading (*see p.37*) also encourages plentiful blooms. Ideal as cut flowers, most, especially those of upright habit, are seen at their best in formal rose beds. Those of bushy habit and thorny growth suit hedging.

Polar Star
Dark glossy leaves and perfect, creamy-white, lightly scented flowers. To 1m.

Warm Wishes ♡
Dark green leaves and peachy salmon-pink blooms with a strong, sweet scent. To 1.1m.

Paul Shirville ♡
Dark glossy leaves, fragrant, high-pointed pink blooms and a spreading habit. To 1m.

◀ OLD GARDEN BEAUTY *Purplish leaves offset the cerise blooms of the species rose R. glauca.*

Lovely Lady ♀
Fragrant, pointed, salmon-
pink blooms and glossy
mid-green leaves. To 75cm.

Double Delight
Sweetly scented, rounded
blooms of creamy-yellow,
flushed carmine. To 1m.

Elina ♀
Dark, red-tinted leaves and
scented, ivory-white flowers
with yellow centres. To 1.1m.

Rosemary Harkness
Glossy, dark leaves, with
sweet-scented, apricot to
salmon-pink flowers. To 80cm.

Fragrant Cloud
Free-flowering, with large,
strongly fragrant, dusky
scarlet blooms. To 75cm.

Just Joey ♀
Large, fragrant, perfectly
shaped, coppery-pink flowers
during summer. To 75cm.

Tequila Sunrise ♀
Scarlet-margined, rich yellow,
lightly scented flowers and
an open habit. To 75cm.

Valencia ♀
Large, high-centred, strongly
fragrant flowers of a rich
amber-yellow. To 75cm.

'Lover's Meeting'
Bronzed leaves and high-
centred, fragrant, reddish-
orange flowers. To 75cm.

MORE CHOICES

FOR FRAGRANCE

Alec's Red Deep crimson
to cherry red
Belle Epoque Golden-bronze
Big Purple Beetroot-purple
'Chrysler Imperial' Deep red
City of London ♀ Pale pink
Indian Summer Creamy-
orange
Peace Yellow, flushed pink
Pot o'Gold Golden-yellow
Royal William Deep crimson
Whisky Mac Pale amber-
yellow

FOR COLOUR

Alexander Vermilion red
Dawn Chorus Rich yellow,
flushed tangerine
'Deep Secret' Rich crimson
Freedom Rich bright yellow
Ingrid Bergman Dark red
Remember Me Copper-
orange
Silver Jubilee Rose-pink,
flushed peach
Solitaire Yellow, edged pink
Velvet Fragrance Deep
velvety crimson

CLUSTER-FLOWERED BUSH ROSES

Intrigue
Purple-green leaves and
dark red flowers. To 70cm.

ALSO KNOWN AS FLORIBUNDAS, cluster-flowered
bush roses have an upright or bushy habit and
produce their often fragrant, single or double flowers
in clusters of 3–25. Most flower repeatedly, almost
continuously through summer and early autumn.
Deadheading (*see p.37*) encourages plentiful blooms;
during the dormant period, they should be pruned
hard (*see p.39*). Many are useful as cut flowers and
are suitable as hedging and in borders. Slightly more
graceful in habit than the large-flowered bushes,
they mix well with other shrubs in a mixed border.

Jacqueline du Pré ♥
Musk-scented, semi-double,
ivory-white flowers. Suitable
for hedging. To 1.5m.

'English Miss'
Clusters of pale pink, camellia-
like blooms. Easy to grow and
good for hedging. To 75cm.

'The Queen Elizabeth' ♥
Dark, glossy leaves and clear
pink flowers. Ideal for cutting
and mixed borders. To 2.2m.

Escapade ♀
Fragrant, white-eyed, pink-violet blooms. Suits cutting and mixed borders. To 75cm.

Trumpeter ♀
Large, bright orange-red flowers, suited to containers and low hedging. To 60cm.

Sheila's Perfume
Fragrant yellow flowers, edged with red. Suits cutting and hedging. To 75cm.

'Korresia'
Fragrant, rich yellow flowers and light foliage for borders and cut flowers. To 75cm.

'Oranges and Lemons'
Scarlet-striped, orange-yellow blooms and dark green leaves, good for borders. To 80cm.

MORE CHOICES

Amber Queen ♀ Scented, amber-yellow
Anisley Dickson ♀ Deep salmon-pink
Anna Livia ♀ Pink
Fellowship Deep orange
Ferdy Rich coral-pink
Iceberg ♀ Creamy-white
Mountbatten ♀ Yellow
Princess Alice Yellow
Sexy Rexy ♀ Rose-pink
'Southampton' ♀ Apricot
The Times Rose ♀ Crimson
Valentine Heart Pink

PATIO AND MINIATURE ROSES

Robin Redbreast
Single, white-centred, dark
red blooms. To 45cm.

PATIO ROSES are dwarf versions of cluster-flowered bush roses and, like them, bear single to double, usually unscented flowers, in clusters throughout the summer. They are perfect for small gardens, as low bedding or in formal borders, and are ideal for growing in containers to decorate a patio or paved area. Miniature roses are similar but even smaller bushes, which also bloom in succession throughout summer. They are suited to containers, for confined spaces, and for edging paths or borders. They can be kept in shape with minimal pruning (*see p.40*).

'White Pet' ♀
Profuse clusters of white,
rosette-form flowers, that are
deep pink in bud. To 45cm.

Queen Mother ♀
Dark green leaves and
clusters of semi-double, soft
clear pink blooms. To 40cm.

Baby Masquerade
Clusters of small, rosette-
form yellow flowers ageing to
pink and crimson. To 40cm.

Little Bo-peep
Short-stemmed, semi-double,
pale pink flowers and dark,
glossy foliage. To 30cm.

'Hula Girl'
Slightly scented, urn-shaped,
pale orange-pink flowers and
glossy foliage. To 50cm.

Anna Ford ♀
Flat, semi-double, orange-red
flowers with a yellow centre.
Dark green leaves. To 45cm.

Orange Sunblaze
Dense, very compact habit
and bright orange-red
blooms. To 30cm.

'Fire Princess'
Rosette-form, bright scarlet
flowers above glossy, dark
green leaves. To 45cm.

Sweet Dream ♔
Fully double, peachy-apricot
flowers above mid-green,
matt leaves. To 40cm.

MORE CHOICES

Bush Baby Salmon-pink
Cider Cup Apricot-pink
'De Meaux' Clear pink
Peek A Boo Apricot-pink
Pretty Polly Rose-pink
Red Ace Deep crimson
Shine On Yellow-apricot
  flushed pink
Sun Hit Clear yellow
Sunseeker Orange-red
Sweet Magic ♔ Apricot-
  orange
Top Marks Deep orange-
  vermilion

Festival
Crimson-scarlet blooms with
silver tints on the petal
reverse. To 60cm.

Boys' Brigade
Clusters of lightly scented,
tiny red flowers, each with
a pale cream eye. To 45cm.

GROUND-COVER ROSES

THESE ROSES have a dense, small-leaved habit; some, such as the "County" roses Hertfordshire and Kent, are spreading and arching; others, such as 'Nozomi', trail along near to the ground, rooting as they go. A few bloom once only, but most flower almost continuously in summer, often wreathing entire stems with single to double, usually unscented, blooms. Use them to cascade over walls and banks, in beds, and at the front of borders. Prune lightly to keep them neat (*see p.40*). Trouble-free and easy to grow, they are also suitable for containers.

Swany ♀
Spreading, with masses of double white flowers. To 75cm.

White Flower Carpet
Very dense habit, with glossy leaves and double, ivory-tinted white flowers. To 60cm.

Kent
Compact and spreading, with clusters of semi-double white flowers. To 45cm.

Pheasant
Low, creeping habit and abundant clusters of rose-pink flowers. To 50cm.

Flower Carpet ♛
Dense, spreading habit and clusters of deep rose-pink flowers. To 75cm.

Cambridgeshire
Semi-double blooms in shades of gold, pink and scarlet. To 45cm.

Hertfordshire
Dense and free-flowering, with single, carmine-pink flowers. To 45cm.

'Nozomi' ♛
Trailing habit, with a single flush of very pale pink flowers in summer. To 45cm.

MORE CHOICES

COUNTY ROSES

Avon White, flushed pale pearly pink with golden stamens
Berkshire Bright cherry pink, with golden stamens
Gwent Lemon-yellow
Northamptonshire Pearly white to pink
Suffolk Bright scarlet with yellow stamens
Surrey ♛ Salmon-pink
Sussex Buff-apricot
Wiltshire Deep reddish-pink

OTHERS

Blenheim White
Bonica ♛ Rose-pink
Broadlands Sulphur yellow
Eyeopener Bright red with yellow eye
La Sévillana Scarlet
Magic Carpet Lilac-pink
'Max Graf' Pink
Pink Bells Bright pink
Red Blanket ♛ Rosy-red
Red Trail Bright red
Rosy Cushion ♛ Pink with white eye

OLD GARDEN AND SPECIES ROSES

'Madame de Sancy
de Parabère'
Blooms early summer. To 5m.

THE OLD ROSES are of European origin, and include some of the most ancient of cultivated roses which have been grown for many centuries. Most bloom once – magnificently – in mid-summer, and are much loved for their divine scents, sumptuous flower form and soft or rich colours, that often take on distinctive tints as they age. They are perfect for mixed borders and as specimens. The species roses, and named selections of the species, are also mostly once-blooming with single or semi-double flowers. Species roses are ideal for natural-style plantings.

'Boule de Neige'
Fragrant, pale pink buds and white flowers repeating throughout summer. To 1.5m.

'Dupontii'
Single, scented, creamy-white flowers borne in a single flush in mid-summer. To 2.2m.

'Frau Karl Druschki'
Vigorous, with milky-white flowers, repeating throughout summer. To 1.5m.

'Stanwell Perpetual'
Fragrant, soft pink flowers repeating in flushes during summer. To 1m.

'Félicité Parmentier' ♥
Fragrant, cream to pale pink flowers borne in a single flush in mid-summer. To 1.2m.

'Great Maiden's Blush'
Very fragrant, with abundant clear pink flowers in a single flush in mid-summer. To 2m.

R. rubiginosa ♀
Apple-scented leaves, pink
blooms borne in a single flush
in mid-summer. To 2.5m.

R. x centifolia 'Muscosa' ♀
Mossy stems, scented, cupped,
pink flowers borne in a single
flush in summer. To 1.5m.

R. gallica var. officinalis
'Versicolor' ♀
Pale pink, red-striped
flowers in summer. To 80cm.

'Président de Sèze' ♀
Scented, pale lilac-pink
flowers packed with petals
during summer. To 1.2m.

'Paul Neyron'
Scented flowers of deep
lilac-tinted pink, repeated in
flushes in summer. To 1.5m.

'Bourbon Queen'
Fragrant, deep rose-pink
flowers, may be repeated in
flushes, in summer. To 2.5m.

'Salet'
Scented, clear pink flowers, occasionally repeated in flushes, in summer. To 1.2m.

'Duc de Guiche' ♀
Rich crimson flowers, scented and packed with petals, borne once in summer. To 1.2m.

'Geranium' ♀
Single, dusky-red blooms in summer, followed by flask-shaped scarlet hips. To 2.5m.

'Empereur du Maroc'
Fragrant flowers of intense deep crimson, may repeat in flushes, in summer. To 1.2m.

'Baron Girod de l'Ain'
Scented crimson flowers with white-lined petals borne throughout summer. To 1.2m.

R. moschata
Musk-scented, single white flowers of summer give rise to orange-red hips. To 3m.

Golden Chersonese
Wreaths of small golden flowers in late spring, above ferny leaves. To 2.2m.

'Reine des Violettes'
Scented, vibrant violet-purple flowers are borne in repeat flushes in summer. To 2m.

MORE CHOICES

'Belle de Crécy' ♀ Fragrant, deep purple-pink
'Cardinal de Richelieu' ♀ Scented, burgundy-purple
'Charles de Mills' ♀ Fragrant, magenta-pink
'Du Maître de l'Ecole' ♀ Purple, ageing to lilac-pink
'Complicata' ♀ Single, pink, pale-centred
R. glauca ♀ Grey-purple foliage and pink flowers
'Zéphirine Drouhin' ♀ Fragrant, deep pink

SHRUB ROSES

Graham Thomas ♀
Fragrant, deep yellow blooms through summer. Up to 1.2m.

THE SHRUB ROSES are a diverse group. Generally larger than bush roses, and often with thorny stems, they have usually scented flowers, from single to fully double, borne singly or in clusters. Most were bred during this century and have the modern characteristic of flowering repeatedly from summer into autumn. Shrub roses are not as tidy as large-flowered bushes and are pruned less rigidly (*see pp.42–3*). They are ideal for mixed borders or as specimens, and many of the dense, robust varieties suit hedging and barrier plantings.

Many Happy Returns ♀
Scented, semi-double, pale pink flowers in showy clusters through summer. To 75cm.

Constance Spry ♀
Myrrh-scented, fully double, pink flowers borne in early to mid-summer. To 2m.

'Roseraie de l'Haÿ' ♀
Scented, double, magenta flowers all summer, and wrinkled leaves. To 2.2m.

Armada
Scented, semi-double, deep pink blooms during summer, and glossy leaves. To 1.5m.

Sally Holmes ♀
Large clusters of scented, single, creamy-white flowers through summer. To 2m.

MORE CHOICES

Abraham Darby Scented, apricot-pink, repeats
'Ballerina' ♀ Single, pale pink with white eye, repeats
Gertrude Jekyll ♀ Fragrant, rich pink, repeats
'Golden Wings' ♀ Single, scented, pale yellow
L.D. Braithwaite Scented, bright crimson, repeats
Mary Rose Fragrant, deep rose-pink, repeats
'The Fairy' ♀ Pale pink, repeats

CLIMBING ROSES

CLIMBING ROSES can be grown on walls, trellis, fences and pillars. A few bloom only once, but most bear flowers repeatedly in summer. Many are scented and their colours and flower forms, whether borne singly or in clusters, are diverse. Climbers generally have stiff, upright growth and produce most of their blooms on sideshoots arising from a woody framework. For the best display, train them carefully in the early years (*see pp.46–7*); otherwise, they grow rapidly upwards, bearing blooms out of reach of both eye and nose.

Dublin Bay ♛
Rich red flowers all summer, and dark leaves. Up to 2.2m.

'Mermaid' ♛
Single, cupped, soft primrose-yellow flowers with golden stamens, in summer. To 6m.

Handel ♛
Stiffly upright growth carries creamy-white flowers with magenta margins. To 3m.

'Aloha'
Sweet-scented rose-pink and salmon-pink flowers throughout summer. To 3m.

Compassion ♛
Fragrant, salmon-pink blooms tinged with apricot produced through summer. To 3m.

Bantry Bay
Semi-double, pale, clear pink flowers with light scent borne throughout summer. To 4m.

Summer Wine ♛
Stiffly upright growth bears single flowers of coral-pink through summer. To 3m.

Dortmund
Clusters of single, white-eyed red flowers borne freely throughout summer. To 3m.

Danse du Feu
Double, rich scarlet flowers in summer, offset against glossy mid-green leaves. To 2.5m.

Sympathie
Glossy leaves bejewelled with fully double, deep red flowers throughout summer. To 3m.

Golden Showers ♀
Fragrant, double, clear yellow blooms borne in clusters throughout summer. To 3m.

'Laura Ford' ♀
Upright, with sweet-scented, semi-double yellow flowers borne in summer. To 2.2m.

MORE CHOICES

'Climbing Arthur Bell' Fragrant, rich yellow

Good as Gold Sweet-scented, golden-yellow

Highfield Large, double, clear yellow

Lavinia Sweet-scented, large, double, pink

Leaping Salmon Strongly scented, soft salmon-pink

'Rosy Mantle' Fragrant, rose- to salmon-pink

Warm Welcome ♀ Semi-double, deep tangerine

RAMBLING ROSES

RAMBLERS differ from climbers in that they tend to produce very long, flexible shoots annually from the base and bear quite spectacular sprays of flowers once only in summer. Many are rampant growers, making them ideal for growing through old trees or over pergolas that hide unsightly garden structures; the flexible stems can also be trained to form swags on ropes. If training on walls, trellis must be set away from the wall to let air circulate freely behind stems; ramblers are prone to powdery mildew, which thrives in warm, stagnant air.

'Albertine' ♀
Scented, salmon-pink flowers in summer. Thorny. To 5m.

'New Dawn' ♀
Softest blush-pink, double flowers are produced all through summer. To 3m.

'Sanders' White Rambler' ♀
Fully double white flowers borne in large clusters in late summer. To 4m.

'Félicité Perpétue' ♀
Small, fully double, pale pink flowers are borne freely during mid-summer. To 5m.

'François Juranville' ♈
Apple-scented, rosette-shaped,
scented, salmon-pink flowers
borne in summer. To 6m.

'Blush Rambler'
Dense clusters of semi-double,
pale pink flowers borne
during late summer. To 4m.

'Seagull' ♈
Wreaths of single white
flowers with golden stamens
in mid-summer. To 6m.

'Crimson Shower' ♈
Cascades of double, crimson
flowers wreathe lax stems all
through summer. To 2.5m.

'Easlea's Golden Rambler'
Small clusters of scented,
apricot-yellow flowers flecked
red, in summer. To 6m.

MORE CHOICES

'Adélaïde d'Orléans' ♈
Lightly scented, semi-
double, pale pink

'Bleu Magenta' ♈ Double,
deep purple with yellow
stamens

'Paul's Himalayan Musk' ♈
Small, double, lilac-pink,
in large sprays

'Phyllis Bide' ♈ Small,
double, buff-pink flushed
yellow, darken with age

'Wedding Day' Fruit-
scented, single, creamy-
white ageing to blush-pink

INDEX

ACKNOWLEDGMENTS

Picture research Neale Chamberlain,
Sam Ruston

Index Hilary Bird

Dorling Kindersley would also like to thank:
Susanne Mitchell, Karen Wilson and Barbara
Haynes at the RHS, Vincent Square.

The Royal Horticultural Society
To learn more about the work of the
Society, visit the RHS on the Internet at
www.rhs.org.uk. Information includes
news of events around the country, a
horticultural database, international plant
registers, results of plant trials and
membership details.

The publisher would like to thank the
following for their kind permission to
reproduce their photographs:
(key: l=left, r=right, b=bottom,
c=centre, t=top)
A-Z Botanical Collection: 66cl. Neil
Campbell-Sharp: jacket front clt, 19tr, 20br,
21tr, 57cl, 69bc. Eric Crichton Photos: 8b,
16b, 18br, 21tl, 23tr, 24b, 61tl, 65cr. Garden
Picture Library: John Glover 61cl. John
Glover: jacket back ct, 6, 7bl, 9br, 14br, 15t,
26cl, 27t, 52, 59bc. Jerry Harpur: 9tl, 14bl,
17tl, 26br. Andrew Lawson: jacket front clb,
18bl, 20bl, 25br. Clive Nichols: Wollerton
Old Hall, Shropshire: 24tl. Photos
Horticultural: 22br. Howard Rice: 2, 10b,
19tl. Harry Smith Collection: 13t